NFL TODAY

THE STORY OF THE
MINNESOTA VIKINGS

THE STORY OF THE MINNESOTA VIKINGS

NATE LEBOUTILLIER

CREATIVE EDUCATION

Cover: Vikings defense, 1969 (top), running back
Adrian Peterson (bottom)
Page 2: Kick returner Aundrae Allison
Pages 4–5: Linebacker Roy Winston
Pages 6–7: Vikings defensive linemen, 1969

....

Published by Creative Education
P.O. Box 227, Mankato, Minnesota 56002
Creative Education is an imprint of
The Creative Company
www.thecreativecompany.us

Design and production by Blue Design
Design Associate: Graham Morgan
Printed in the United States of America

Photographs by Getty Images (Brian Bahr, Doug
Benc, Andrew D. Bernstein, Vernon Biever/NFL, Paul
Buck/AFP, Tom Dahlin, Jonathan Daniel/Allsport,
Tom DiPace/Sports Illustrated, James Flores/
NFL Photos, Focus On Sport, Drew Hallowell, Tom
Hauck, Walter Iooss Jr./Sports Illustrated, Kidwiler
Collection/Diamond Images, Heinz Kluetmeier/
Sports Illustrated, Andy Lyons/Allsport, John
Mabanglo/AFP, Martin Morrow/NFL Photos, Ronald
C. Modra/Sports Imagery, Mike Nelson/AFP, NFL,
Manny Rubio/NFL, Ryan/Beyer, Robert Sullivan/AFP,
Rob Tringali/Sportschrome)

Library of Congress Cataloging-in-Publication Data

LeBoutillier, Nate.
The story of the Minnesota Vikings / by Nate
LeBoutillier.
p. cm. — (NFL today)
Includes index.
ISBN 978-1-58341-762-1
1. Minnesota Vikings (Football team)—History—
Juvenile literature. I. Title. II. Series.

GV956.M5L43 2009
796.332'6409776579—dc22   2008022693

First Edition
9 8 7 6 5 4 3 2 1

CONTENTS

THE SHIP EMBARKS..........................8

THE GOLDEN (AND PURPLE) YEARS 20

THE GREEN ERA 28

RE-RIGHTING THE SHIP...................36

INDEX 48

ON THE SIDELINES

WRONG WAY JIM............................ 12

COLD-FIELD ADVANTAGE.................... 16

SAN FRANCISCO STUNNER.................. 24

HIGH-POWERED HEARTBREAK 33

TRAINING CAMP TRAGEDY 41

BIG DAY FOR "ALL DAY" 45

MEET THE VIKINGS

BUD GRANT 11

ALAN PAGE 15

FRAN TARKENTON 27

CHUCK FOREMAN........................... 30

JOHN RANDLE 38

CRIS CARTER............................... 46

THE SHIP EMBARKS

X--------------------------------

With the lowest average temperature of any of the major metropolitan areas in the United States, Minneapolis-St. Paul is used to the cold. The whole state of Minnesota is chilly, especially in winter, but its residents have ways of dealing with it. From the first American Indians to early settlers of the 1800s to citizens of today, those who have made their home in Minnesota have adapted and toughened. In fact, by participating in such winter activities as ice fishing, hunting, skating, skiing, snowmobiling, and good old-fashioned snowball fights, they even choose to celebrate the cold.

X In the past half century, the city of Minneapolis—founded along the mighty Mississippi River—has earned a reputation for both its rich artistic culture and its great sports tradition.

Since 1961, Minnesotans have also gathered in fall and winter to cheer on a team in the National Football League (NFL). That year, a new franchise built from scratch settled in the "Twin Cities" area of Minneapolis and St. Paul. In a way, this new team replaced Minnesota's first major professional sports team, basketball's Minneapolis Lakers, which played in the state from 1947 to 1960 before moving to Los Angeles. The new club was named the Vikings—tough, pirate-like sailors from Scandinavia, another northern region across the Atlantic Ocean—and was prepared to ransack the NFL.

It is fitting that the Vikings' history begins with a man named Winter—Max Winter. In the late 1950s, the Minnesota businessman sought to establish a football

franchise in his home state and began writing letters to the NFL commissioner. In 1960, the league finally gave in to his repeated requests, and the Vikings were born.

Winter hired Norm Van Brocklin, a former NFL quarterback known for his short temper, as the team's first head coach. The original Vikings roster was made up mostly of unproven rookies and veterans cast off by other teams. Among the veterans was former San Francisco 49ers star running back Hugh McElhenny, and the rookies included running back Tommy Mason, cornerback Ed Sharockman, and quarterback Fran Tarkenton.

No one expected much of the first-year Vikings in their inaugural 1961 season, but they opened eyes around the league by crushing the Chicago Bears 37–13 in their first game. In the victory, Tarkenton proved himself a rising star by passing for four touchdowns and running for another. The Vikings went 3–11 that first season and posted losing records their next few as well, but Tarkenton's scrambling style never failed to thrill fans—and irritate his old-fashioned coach. Tarkenton had his reasons for darting around in the backfield. "Why should I stand there and get broken in two?" he once said. "If I run, there's always a chance that I will find a receiver."

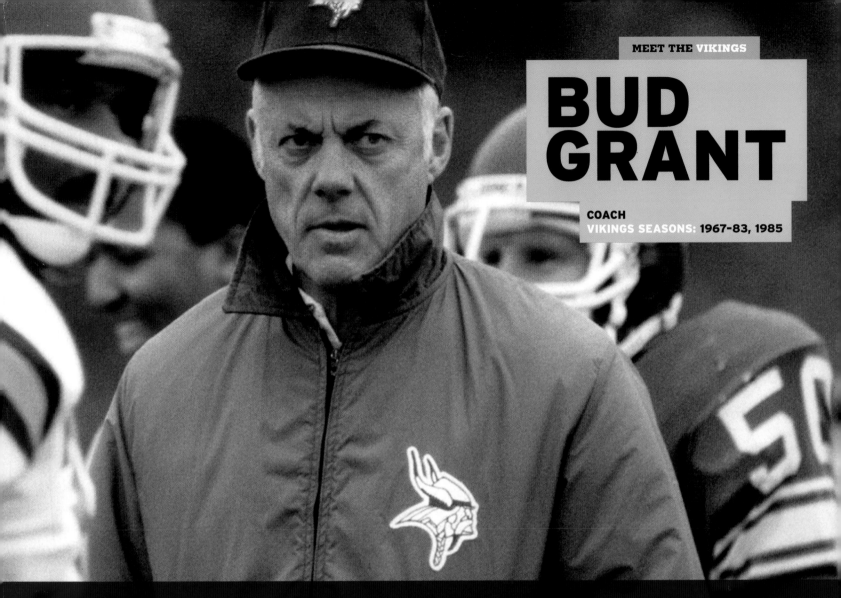

BUD GRANT

COACH
VIKINGS SEASONS: 1967-83, 1985

As head coach of the Minnesota Vikings for 18 seasons, Bud Grant created an air of stability and success that many franchises coveted. While his four trips to the Super Bowl and 168–108–5 win-loss record speak for themselves, the sheer presence of Grant—calm-eyed and confident—on the Minnesota sidelines was probably most impressive. Grant was a terrific athlete before he became a coach, as he starred in baseball, basketball, and football at the University of Minnesota in the late 1940s. He played basketball professionally for the Minneapolis Lakers for two years, then turned to football, playing offensive and defensive end for two years with the Philadelphia Eagles and later moving on to the Winnipeg Blue Bombers of the Canadian Football League. After much success in Winnipeg, Grant was recruited to coach the Vikings, and his teams became known for their toughness and no-nonsense demeanor. Grant was elected to the Pro Football Hall of Fame in 1994. "He has so much common sense," Vikings kicker Jan Stenerud once said. "Most of us have common sense the next day, but Bud has it before a thing happens."

WRONG WAY JIM

When Minnesota Vikings defensive end Jim Marshall got spun around and rambled for his famous "Wrong Way Run," dizzy people everywhere could relate. "Think of the worst thing you've ever done," said Marshall, "the thing you're most ashamed of—and it was seen by 80 million people. Then think of people coming up to you and reminding you of it for the rest of your life." The scene of Marshall's folly was San Francisco, California, in a game against the 49ers, on October 25, 1964. Marshall scooped up a 49ers fumble and, disoriented, began to hoof it in the wrong direction. Some of Marshall's Vikings teammates pursued him but couldn't catch up or get his attention. Marshall sprinted into the 49ers' end zone and celebrated his jaunt by happily winging the ball into the stands. The resulting safety cost the Vikings two points, but Marshall offset the mistake by causing another 49ers fumble that the Vikings returned for a touchdown in a 27–22 victory. What's more, Marshall would eventually become the all-time NFL leader in opponents' fumble recoveries with 29.

While the Vikings' exciting offense showed promise, the defense needed work. One of the few bright spots was defensive end Don Hultz. In 1963, the rookie earned league-wide attention by recovering nine opponents' fumbles—an NFL single-season record. His Vikings teammates began calling him "The Magnet," but Hultz stayed humble. "I just happen to be there when another one of our guys is shaking somebody up," he explained.

Hultz was soon traded away to make room in the lineup for Carl Eller, another outstanding young defensive end. But the defense was truly anchored in Minnesota's early years by Jim Marshall. One of the original Vikings, the 6-foot-4 and 248-pound end seemed indestructible; he would spend 19 seasons with the Vikings and play in an NFL-record 282 consecutive games. Although his career featured countless highlights, many fans will always remember a famous "lowlight" that took place in 1964. In a game against the San Francisco 49ers that season, Marshall scooped up a fumble and, confused, raced the wrong direction into the end zone, giving the 49ers two points for a safety.

With the emergence of tough running backs Bill Brown and Tommy Mason, center Mick Tinglehoff, and kicker Fred Cox, the Vikings slowly improved, going 8–5–1 in 1964. Then problems developed on the sidelines. Coach Van Brocklin and Tarkenton often clashed, and the losses started piling up again.

Following a 4–9–1 season in 1966, Van Brocklin became more and more agitated with Tarkenton's maverick style, saying, "There are two types of quarterbacks—those who carry a team and those who have to be carried by the team. Francis will win some games he shouldn't win, but he'll lose some games he shouldn't lose." In 1967, Tarkenton was traded away to the New York Giants for four draft picks and cash, and Van Brocklin resigned.

Max Winter chose Bud Grant as the team's next head coach. A former football and baseball standout at the University of Minnesota—and a former coach in the Canadian Football League—Grant was just the patient, determined leader the Vikings needed. A tall, stern figure with a steely gaze, he would remain the face of the Minnesota Vikings for 18 seasons.

In 1968, Grant and the Vikings won their first and only NFL Central Division title with an 8–6 record. Part of the credit went to scrappy signal-caller Joe Kapp, who steadied the Vikings' attack with more traditional quarterback play; safety Paul Krause, who guided the defense with his on-field smarts and seven interceptions; and rookie Bobby Bryant, who made

ALAN PAGE

DEFENSIVE TACKLE
VIKINGS SEASONS: 1967-78
HEIGHT: 6-FOOT-4
WEIGHT: 245 POUNDS

It took only four games for Alan Page to win a starting role at defensive tackle with the Minnesota Vikings in his rookie season. For the next 12 seasons, Page never looked back, stuffing ballcarriers and sacking quarterbacks with his nimbleness and a game built on quickness and smarts. In 1971, Page became just the second defensive player in NFL history to win the league's Most Valuable Player (MVP) award. That season, Page recorded 9 sacks, 65 tackles, and generally terrorized opposing offenses. Page was also a four-time Defensive Player of the Year in the National Football Conference (NFC), and along with fellow "Purple People Eaters" Jim Marshall and Carl Eller, he helped the Vikings reach four Super Bowls from 1970 to 1977. For his career, he blocked an incredible 28 kicks and recovered 23 fumbles. Page became a shining role model for ex-athletes when he retired from football, gained a law degree, and in 1992 was elected as an Associate Justice of the Minnesota Supreme Court, becoming the first African American to ever serve on that court. He was re-elected in 1998 and 2004.

ON THE SIDELINES

COLD-FIELD ADVANTAGE

Many people can't stand the cold weather in the state of Minnesota. The Minnesota Vikings, early in their history, used that to their advantage. From 1961 to 1981, when the weather turned cold, the Vikings were nearly unstoppable as icy winds and freezing temperatures blew through Metropolitan Stadium. Their coach, Bud Grant, made sure they were ready for the cold by always making the team practice outdoors and prohibiting certain comforts such as heaters or gloves. The result was an emphatic home-field advantage that helped the Vikings compile a 97–59–4 record in "The Met" against their often-shivering opponents. The fans, decked out in warm winter gear, loved it. But the NFL eventually declared Metropolitan Stadium's seating capacity too small, and in 1982, the Vikings moved indoors to the Metrodome. They developed a home-field advantage of a different sort when the screaming crowd would deafen opponents by using their outdoor voices. But many Minnesota fans miss their football in the snow, and in 2005, new Vikings owner Zygi Wilf announced a desire to eventually move the team back outside.

a solid impression at cornerback and would remain in the Vikings' defensive backfield for the next 13 seasons.

But the brightest stars were on the defensive line. Made up of ends Marshall and Eller and tackles Alan Page and Gary Larsen, Minnesota's line was among the NFL's best. All four players were amazingly quick and relentless in their pursuit. This fearsome front four, which became known as the "Purple People Eaters," followed a simple game plan: "Meet at the quarterback."

In 1969, the Vikings set sail for greatness. Kapp torched the Baltimore Colts with an NFL-record seven touchdown passes in the second game of the season. The Vikings won 12 games in a row before beating the Cleveland Browns 27–7 in the NFL Championship Game to win their first league title. As NFL champs, the Vikings then took on the Kansas City Chiefs of the rival American Football League (AFL) in Super Bowl IV. (Prior to the 1970 season, when the AFL and NFL merged, the NFL champs played the AFL champs in the Super Bowl.) The Vikings were heavily favored, but they could never get their offense going and lost 23–7.

X The main four members of the famed and feared "Purple People Eaters" line played together in Vikings purple for eight seasons.

THE GOLDEN (AND PURPLE) YEARS

X ------------

X Combining
his always-exciting
scrambles with 18
seasons' worth of
passes, Fran Tarkenton
accounted for 50,677
yards—about 29 miles—
of total offense in his
NFL career.

Despite the upset in Super Bowl IV, the good times were just starting in Minnesota. The Vikings ruled the new NFC Central throughout the 1970s, winning the division eight times. In 1972, to the delight of many fans, Tarkenton returned and resumed scrambling across the frozen turf of Metropolitan Stadium. In 1975, Tarkenton—whom Grant called "the greatest quarterback ever in the NFL"—threw 25 touchdown passes and was named the league's MVP. With Tarkenton, running back Chuck Foreman, and wide receiver John Gilliam leading a strong offense, and with the Purple People Eaters continuing to devour opponents, the Vikings went 45–10–1 from 1973 to 1976 and returned to the Super Bowl three more times. Sadly, the biggest prize of all eluded them, as they lost each time.

In 1975, the Vikings might have had their best squad of the era, going 12–2 in the regular season. But Minnesota, heavily favored to reach the Super Bowl, lost 17–14 to the Dallas Cowboys in the NFC playoffs when Cowboys receiver Drew Pearson hauled in a 50-yard scoring bomb from quarterback

X The Vikings surrendered fewer yards than any other team in football in 1975, the season that ended with the controversial Drew Pearson reception.

Roger Staubach with just 24 seconds remaining. The Vikings, and many Minnesota fans, contended that Pearson illegally pushed off of Vikings cornerback Nate Wright, and replays showed they might have been correct in their grievance.

As the 1970s drew to a close, the Vikings were haunted by their Super Bowl losses: 23–7 to Kansas City in Super Bowl IV; 24–7 to the Miami Dolphins in Super Bowl VIII; 16–6 to the Pittsburgh Steelers in Super Bowl IX; and 32–14 to the Oakland Raiders in Super Bowl XI. Although they would get close, the Vikings would not return to the Super Bowl during the next three decades.

X Halfback Chuck Foreman's lanky frame made him a big target for tacklers, but his quick moves made him tough to bring down in the open field.

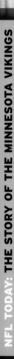

SAN FRANCISCO STUNNER

The Vikings have won their share of playoff games—18 of them through 2008—but none were more improbable than a 36–24 win over the San Francisco 49ers following the 1987 season. The Vikings were 11-point underdogs to the 49ers, who finished the regular season 13–2 and were led by legendary quarterback Joe Montana and receiver Jerry Rice. Minnesota finished just 8–7 in the regular season but stomped the New Orleans Saints 44–10 in the playoffs' first round. Playing in drizzly conditions in San Francisco, the Vikings jumped out to a 27–10 lead, causing 49ers coach Bill Walsh to actually bench Montana. Anthony Carter (pictured), an underused third-year Vikings receiver, caught 10 passes for an NFL playoff-record 227 yards, and—boosted by kicker Chuck Nelson's five field goals—the Vikings had their upset. Afterward, everyone raved about Carter's performance. "Anything you threw out there, he went and got it," said Vikings coach Jerry Burns. "He took the ball away from people. That was the most sensational one particular game that I've ever seen any receiver play."

Before the exodus of many of the great Vikings players who tasted success in the '70s, a memorable game unfolded during the 1980 season. In the second-to-last game of the regular season, the Vikings needed a win over the Cleveland Browns to capture the NFC Central. Down 23–22, the Vikings had the ball at midfield. Minnesota quarterback Tommy Kramer launched a hopeful pass toward the end zone as time expired, and the ball ricocheted off five different players before settling into the hands of receiver Ahmad Rashad, giving the Vikings an improbable 28–23 victory. The play became known in team lore as "The Miracle Catch."

The 1982 opening of the Hubert H. Humphrey Metrodome, an indoor stadium with a fiberglass roof, signaled the start of a new era for the Vikings. Old Metropolitan Stadium was torn down, and most of the team's former stars were soon replaced by a new band of Vikings.

Minnesota was a mediocre team for much of the 1980s. Kramer quarterbacked the offense for many of those seasons, while the defense was led by linebacker Scott Studwell, tough safety Joey Browner, and defensive end Chris Doleman. Coach Grant intended to retire after the 1983 season, but after new coach Les Steckel's 1984 team stumbled to a 3–13 mark, Grant returned for a final season in 1985 before stepping down for good.

Perhaps no Vikings player shone as brightly in the late '80s as receiver Anthony Carter. Carter joined Minnesota in 1985 after an amazing college career at the University of Michigan. Although he stood only 5-foot-11 and weighed just 169 pounds, Carter made up for his lack of size with terrific instincts and quickness. He also showed surprising speed, often streaking downfield to haul in long-range bombs. "I've always said that if the good Lord put anybody on this earth to play pro football, it was A. C.," said coach Jerry Burns, who took over for Grant in 1986. "He just forgot to give him a body."

Carter's heroics and a tough defense helped the Vikings make the playoffs in 1987, 1988, and 1989. In the 1987 playoffs, the 8–7 Vikings stunned the sports world by beating the New Orleans Saints 44–10 and the San Francisco 49ers 36–24 to reach the NFC Championship Game. The title game against the Washington Redskins was a close battle, but Minnesota fell just short of the Super Bowl. The Vikings appeared ready to tie the game when Minnesota quarterback Wade Wilson fired a short pass to running back Darrin Nelson in the end zone late in the fourth quarter. But the ball slipped through Nelson's hands, giving the Redskins a 17–10 victory that propelled them to a Super Bowl title one game later.

FRAN TARKENTON

QUARTERBACK
VIKINGS SEASONS: 1961-66, 1972-78
HEIGHT: 6 FEET
WEIGHT: 185 POUNDS

In the first game in Minnesota Vikings history, Fran Tarkenton, a wiry rookie quarterback from Georgia, came off the bench to sling four touchdowns and run for a fifth as the Vikings toppled the Chicago Bears, 37–13. Tarkenton made a name for himself as a scrambling renegade whose dazzling escapes from the clutches of would-be tacklers had fans holding their breath. Not that he never took a hit. "It's kind of peaceful down there," Tarkenton said about occasionally ending up underneath a pile of tacklers. "It's a good time to be planning your next play." In 1967, Minnesota traded its star to the New York Giants. However, the Vikings re-acquired Tarkenton in 1972. Tarkenton's second tour of duty for the purple and gold was much more successful, as he led the Vikings to three Super Bowls before he retired. After 18 seasons of football, Tarkenton was the all-time NFL leader in most significant passing categories, including touchdowns (342), completions (3,686), and yards (47,003). He also rushed for 3,674 yards in his career, easily the best ever for a quarterback at that time.

THE GREEN ERA

In 1992, the Vikings brought in former Stanford University coach Dennis Green as their new leader. At the time, the Vikings were best known for their defense. Luckily, Minnesota had just acquired a player Coach Green could build a mighty offense around, too: wide receiver Cris Carter.

Carter had been a good player with the Philadelphia Eagles, but he had also struggled with drug and alcohol problems, and the Eagles cut him in 1990. Carter's lanky frame and terrific hands enabled him to catch virtually any pass, and his confident and vocal personality made him essentially a coach on the field. In 1994, he set a new NFL record with 122 catches, many of them on high, "alley-oop" passes. "I always tell the quarterback, when in doubt, just throw it high, and I'll go up and get it," Carter said.

Green and Carter led the Vikings back to power as Minnesota made the playoffs every year but one between 1992 and 2000, winning the NFC Central four times. A number of players contributed to these good times. Robert Smith, a

If a pass was close enough to touch, Cris Carter usually caught it; in both 1994 and 1995, the 8-time Pro-Bowler famed for his catching dexterity hauled in an incredible 122 passes. **X**-----

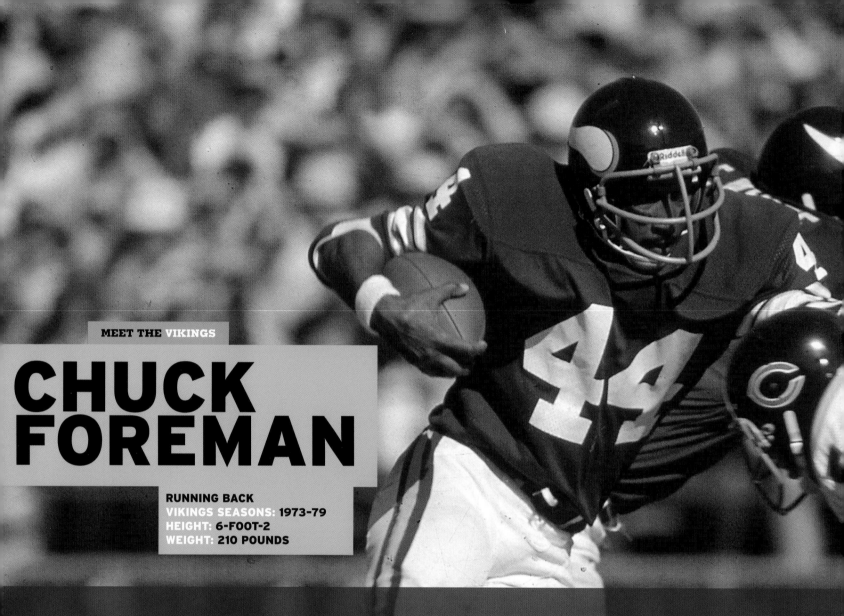

CHUCK FOREMAN

RUNNING BACK
VIKINGS SEASONS: 1973-79
HEIGHT: 6-FOOT-2
WEIGHT: 210 POUNDS

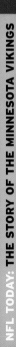

Silky-smooth moves and an upright running posture that netted big gains was the signature style of running back Chuck Foreman, who wore number 44 for the Minnesota Vikings in the 1970s. A native of Maryland, Foreman starred in three sports in high school: basketball, track and field, and, of course, football. The kind of athletic ability that enabled him to excel at three sports made Foreman a dual threat to either catch or run on the gridiron. In 1973, Foreman burst onto the scene and was voted NFC Offensive Rookie of the Year as the Vikings made it all the way to Super Bowl VIII. The Vikings rode him to three Super Bowls in their glory days, and although Foreman's career was cut short by knee injuries, he put up some great performances. In 1975, Foreman scored 22 touchdowns (13 on the ground and 9 through the air), rushed for 1,070 yards, and led the entire league in pass receptions with 73. But what fans remember best were the breathtaking spin moves and jitterbugging jaunts that so often led Foreman to the end zone.

long-striding running back with great speed, was drafted in 1993 and went on to average more than 1,000 yards a season throughout the rest of the '90s. Various quarterbacks came and went during the Green era, but in 1994, veteran passer Warren Moon joined the Vikings and set a new team record by throwing for 4,264 yards. On the defensive side of the ball, powerful and eccentric tackle John Randle was a nightmare for opposing quarterbacks, while hard-hitting linebackers Jack Del Rio and Ed McDaniel punished ballcarriers.

Making the playoffs was one thing, but reaching the Super Bowl was another. The Vikings lost in the first round of the playoffs every year until 1997. Then, in one of the most thrilling games in franchise history, quarterback Randall Cunningham helped turn a 19–3 halftime deficit to the New York Giants into a stunning 23–22 victory. The Vikings were beaten a week later, but even better things were just around the corner.

In 1998, the Vikings franchise was bought by Texas billionaire Red McCombs. The new owner introduced "Purple Pride" as the team's new battle cry, and he boldly predicted that Minnesota would go a perfect 16–0. Fortunately, the Vikings had just added a rookie receiver who would almost make that a reality: Randy Moss. Moss stood 6-foot-4, and his

X With rookie wideout Randy Moss on board, the Vikings offense flew to new heights in 1998, scoring more than 40 points in 4 different games and rewriting numerous NFL records.

otherworldly speed and jumping ability had earned him the nickname "The Freak." "Moss is the scariest man in football and the best player, talent-wise," Green Bay Packers coach Mike Sherman said. "You hold your breath every time they snap the ball."

Minnesota didn't go 16–0 as McCombs had predicted, but it came close. The 1998 Vikings went 15–1 and set a new NFL record with 556 total points. Moss was especially spectacular, posting 1,313 receiving yards and scoring 17 receiving touchdowns—the latter a new league record for a rookie. In

HIGH-POWERED HEARTBREAK

The 1998 Vikings offense had it all: a powerful line, the rushing of former track star Robert Smith (pictured), and a passing game featuring rejuvenated quarterback Randall Cunningham, sure-handed receiver Cris Carter, and fleet-footed rookie phenom Randy Moss. Even the Vikings' kicker, Gary Anderson, couldn't miss—he became the first NFL kicker to post a perfect season, not missing one of his 35 attempted field goals or 59 extra-point kicks. In all, the offensive juggernaut scored a then-league-record 556 points and breezed through the regular season with a 15–1 mark. The Vikings thumped the Arizona Cardinals 41–21 in the first round of the playoffs and prepared to down the Atlanta Falcons to reach the Super Bowl. But the Falcons, 11-point underdogs, would not be blown out. Anderson had a 38-yard field goal try in the fourth quarter to seal the victory, but he finally missed a kick, and the Falcons forced overtime and converted a field goal for a 30–27 win. "Our offense was supposed to have been so explosive," said Moss, who had just one catch after halftime. "But we just couldn't make it happen in the clutch."

the playoffs, the Vikings crushed the Arizona Cardinals 41–21 to reach the NFC Championship Game.

Playing in front of a deafening Metrodome crowd, the Vikings raced to a 20–7 lead over the Atlanta Falcons. But Minnesota's offense then sputtered, and the Falcons clawed their way back to tie the game at 27–27. In sudden-death overtime, Atlanta stopped the Vikings offense before kicking a game-winning field goal. The Vikings and their fans were devastated. "The Super Bowl is something you dream of as a kid," Moss said sadly, "and we had an opportunity to get there. . . . We let it slip right out of our hands." The Vikings had reached the Super Bowl four times only to lose it in the 1970s, but this loss might have been the most disappointing ever for fans of the purple and gold.

X Even the ear-splitting, home-field advantage of the Metrodome could not prevent the 1998 NFC Championship Game from becoming another big-game heartbreak for Vikings fans.

X The 1998 season was quarterback Randall Cunningham's one great hurrah in Minnesota; in the nine other combined games he started in 1997 and 1999, he went a mere 3–6.

RE-RIGHTING
THE SHIP

Minnesota rebounded from the painful defeat by making

the playoffs again the next two seasons. In 2000, behind

the great play of young quarterback Daunte Culpepper—a

6-foot-4 and 260-pound threat to either launch the ball deep

downfield or steamroller linebackers or defensive backs—

Minnesota fought its way back to the NFC Championship

Game. But in one of the worst performances in team history,

the Vikings were obliterated 41–0 by the Giants. Soon after

this embarrassing loss, a number of key leaders left town

or retired. Among the departures were Minnesota's all-time

rushing leader (Robert Smith), its all-time pass-catching

leader (Cris Carter), and Coach Green.

A new era dawned as Mike Tice, a former Vikings

tight end, was named the team's head coach. Tice instituted

a new offensive theory for the 2002 season called "The Randy

Ratio," which called for Moss, the team's brightest star, to

touch the ball on at least 40 percent of all offensive plays.

Unfortunately, the plan fell flat as opposing teams focused

on stopping Moss, who had an impressive 106 catches but

only 7 touchdowns in the Vikings' 6–10 season.

With an offense that featured Moss and Culpepper—

and with a defense anchored by powerful young tackle

Kevin Williams—the Vikings remained a dangerous team in

X Defending against Daunte Culpepper was a serious challenge; besides his enormous size and fast feet, he consistently ranked among the NFL's most accurate passers.

JOHN RANDLE

DEFENSIVE TACKLE
VIKINGS SEASONS: 1990–2000
HEIGHT: 6-FOOT-1
WEIGHT: 290 POUNDS

If pure energy could have been embodied on the NFL gridiron in the 1990s, it would have donned black face paint, worn a purple number 93 jersey, and doggedly chased down quarterbacks. It would have looked exactly like John Randle. A disruptive, duck-walking, body-slamming force who ran his mouth at opponents all game long, Randle was a quarterback's worst nightmare. From his position on the defense's interior line, Randle infused hustle and comedy into Vikings teams that usually featured powerful offense and shaky defense. Randle developed a coyote-roadrunner relationship with Green Bay Packers quarterback Brett Favre, whom he sacked numerous times. In a memorable television commercial, Randle chased a chicken wearing a number 4 Packers jersey across his lawn before a final scene that showed him grilling chicken for dinner. But for all his acting, Randle did have serious substance. He was a seven-time Pro-Bowler and finished his career with 137.5 sacks, the most of any defensive tackle in NFL history—quite an accomplishment for a player who went undrafted by the league coming out of college.

the new NFC North Division (which was formed in 2002). In 2004, Culpepper enjoyed a career year, setting Vikings single-season records for passing with 4,717 total yards and 39 touchdowns, and setting an NFL record for total yards running and passing with 5,123. Minnesota made the playoffs despite a mediocre 8–8 record, then traveled to Green Bay to face the archrival Packers and their star quarterback, Brett Favre.

That game ended with one of the most satisfying Vikings victories in years, as Minnesota earned a lopsided 31–17 win despite having lost both regular-season games

X In 2003, three years after John Randle left town, Kevin Williams (pictured) emerged as the next great Vikings defensive tackle.

Randy Moss styled his hair up into a wild Afro for the Vikings' playoff win over the Packers after the 2004 season—a game that turned out to be one of his last in a Minnesota uniform. **X**

to Green Bay. Moss again stole headlines in a performance that epitomized his Vikings career. After making a late fourth-quarter touchdown catch, he taunted the Packers crowd by pretending to lower his pants and show his backside. That was to be Moss's final noteworthy game in a purple jersey. The Vikings lost in the next round to the Philadelphia Eagles. Then, tired of the star receiver's disruptive antics, Minnesota traded Moss away to the Oakland Raiders.

TRAINING CAMP TRAGEDY

Six years into his career as an offensive tackle for the Vikings, Korey Stringer was finally developing into the dominant player Minnesota had hoped for when it drafted him in 1995 out of Ohio State University. But on July 31, 2001, that development stopped forever. The 6-foot-5 and 350-pound Stringer, fighting his poor fitness level, weight, and an especially wicked late summer heat wave, suffered a heatstroke and collapsed at the Vikings' training camp in Mankato, Minnesota. He was taken to a medical tent and later rushed to a hospital but never responded to cool-down treatment. Stringer died early the next morning, leaving his family, teammates, and Minnesota fans in shock. The temperature was 90-plus degrees with high humidity, but NFL players had often dealt with such weather conditions. "It's hot everywhere," said Vikings receiver Cris Carter. "That's why they call it the dog days of summer. There's certain things you can't explain." Since the incident, teams league-wide have taken better heat precautions by practicing in light-colored uniforms, making water and shade more readily available, and always having a doctor on the field.

After the 2005 Vikings missed the playoffs, both Culpepper and Coach Tice were shown the door by new team owner Zygi Wilf, and former Eagles assistant coach Brad Childress was hired as the new head coach. His first season at the helm yielded just a 6–10 record, but in 2007, the Vikings defense, led by cornerback Antoine Winfield, showed signs of dominance. The team contended for a postseason berth until the season's final week, finishing with an 8–8 mark.

Although the Vikings' 2007 season ended shy of the playoffs, it did showcase two new offensive weapons: second-year quarterback Tarvaris Jackson, and rookie running back Adrian Peterson. While Jackson showed flashes of excellence, Peterson was an instant sensation. A former star at the University of Oklahoma, he boasted a rare combination of power, cutting ability, and breakaway speed. By the end of the year, he had become the new face of the franchise and earned NFL Offensive Rookie of the Year honors.

Before the start of the 2008 season, the Vikings made headlines by trading for Kansas City Chiefs defensive end Jared Allen, the NFL's sack leader in 2007. With the relentless Allen placed alongside Pro Bowl tackles Kevin Williams and Pat Williams, Vikings fans started dreaming of a return to the days of the Purple People Eaters. The confident Allen was direct in

X Halfback Adrian Peterson cut a heroic figure as just a rookie in 2007; despite missing 2 games with an injury, he galloped for 1,341 yards, many of them in highlight fashion.

The Vikings' acquisition of Jared Allen was big news in 2008, as his $74-million contract made him the richest defensive player in NFL history. **X**

stating his goals upon arrival, saying, "We expect to go to the Super Bowl." Allen then backed up his words by notching 14.5 sacks as the 2008 Vikings went 10–6 and won their first NFC North title. In the playoffs, though, not even the efforts of Allen and Peterson—the NFL's rushing champ with 1,760 yards—could lift Minnesota above Philadelphia, as the Vikings lost 26–14.

BIG DAY FOR "ALL DAY"

Success came early for halfback Adrian Peterson, the Vikings' first-round draft choice in 2007. Just eight games into his pro football career, he broke the NFL's single-game rushing record by amassing 296 yards against the San Diego Chargers on November 4, 2007. Although he had been used somewhat sparingly by the Vikings' coaching staff in the season's first 5 games, Peterson had a breakout game with 224 yards and 3 touchdowns in a win versus the Chicago Bears in Week 6. Against the Chargers, who boasted one of the league's top defenses, Peterson went ballistic. After he rushed for 43 yards and a touchdown in the first half, with his team losing 14–7, the Vikings turned loose the man known as "All Day" in the second half. Resembling the lighting bolts depicted on his opponents' helmets, Peterson spun, juked, and sprinted his way to two more long touchdowns and into the record books as the Vikings won, 35–17. "I was out playing ball," Peterson explained after the game. "I wasn't thinking about the record at all."

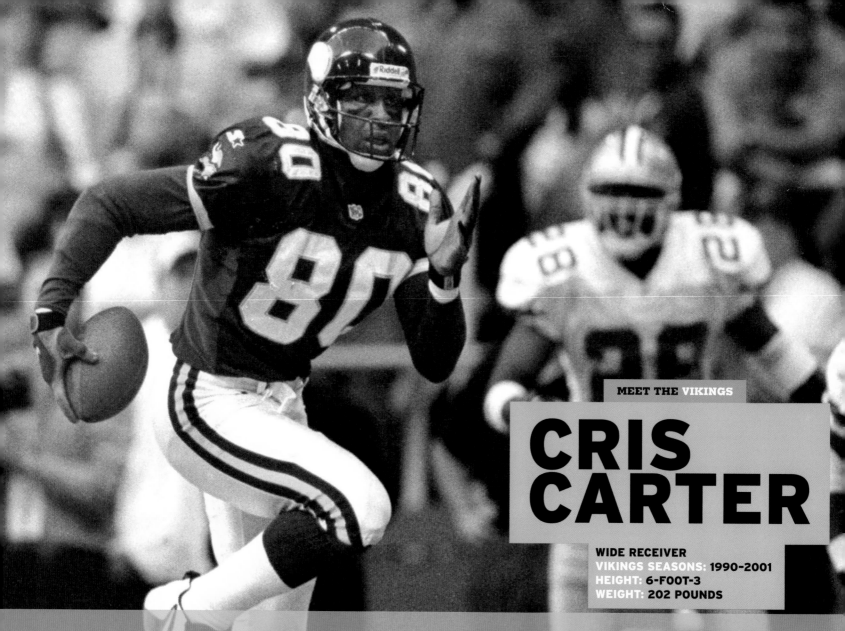

CRIS CARTER

WIDE RECEIVER
VIKINGS SEASONS: 1990-2001
HEIGHT: 6-FOOT-3
WEIGHT: 202 POUNDS

Cris Carter's career almost ended before it even had a chance to begin. Carter came into the NFL out of Ohio State University with some baggage because he had been ruled ineligible for his senior season after having secretly signed with an agent. The Philadelphia Eagles picked him up in the NFL Draft and used him somewhat sparingly, even though Carter showed a knack for getting into the end zone, with 19 of his 89 career receptions as an Eagles player going for scores. In the 1990 preseason, Eagles coach Buddy Ryan cut Carter, saying, "All he does is catch touchdowns." That didn't sound so bad to the Minnesota Vikings, who claimed him for just a $100 waiver fee. In Minnesota, Carter turned his life around—freeing himself from substance abuse problems and becoming deeply religious—and earned a reputation for his acrobatic sideline catches and clutch, third-down receptions. With his sure hands, he continued to do what he did best—catch touchdowns. Carter finished his career with 130 touchdowns, second-most all-time among receivers behind 49ers great Jerry Rice.

The story of the Minnesota Vikings is one of success—and heartache. Although the team has won 18 playoff games since its inception in 1961, it has suffered painful losses in 4 Super Bowls and 4 NFC Championship Games. As today's Vikings continue their voyage toward a Super Bowl victory, they will continue to make those cold game days in the snowy North seem a little bit warmer.

Minnesota fans hoped that Ragnar, the Vikings' team mascot, would soon be leading a world championship team onto the field. **X**

INDEX

Allen, Jared 43, 44

Anderson, Gary 33

Brown, Bill 13

Browner, Joey 25

Bryant, Bobby 14, 17

Burns, Jerry 24, 26

Carter, Anthony 24, 26

Carter, Cris 28, 33, 37, 41, 46

Childress, Brad 43

Cox, Fred 13

Culpepper, Daunte 37, 39, 43

Cunningham, Randall 31, 33

Defensive Player of the Year award 15

Del Rio, Jack 31

division championships 14, 21, 28, 44

Doleman, Chris 25

Eller, Carl 13, 15, 17

first season 10

Foreman, Chuck 21, 30

Gilliam, John 21

Grant, Bud 11, 14, 16, 21, 25, 26

Green, Dennis 28, 31, 37

Hultz, Don 13

Jackson, Tarvaris 43

Kapp, Joe 14, 17

Kramer, Tommy 25

Krause, Paul 14

Larsen, Gary 17

Marshall, Jim 12, 13, 15, 17

Mason, Tommy 10, 13

McCombs, Red 31, 32

McDaniel, Ed 31

McElhenny, Hugh 10

Metrodome 16, 25, 35

Metropolitan Stadium 16, 21, 25

Moon, Warren 31

Moss, Randy 31–32, 33, 35, 37, 40

MVP award 15, 21

Nelson, Chuck 24

Nelson, Darrin 26

NFC Championship Game 26, 35, 37, 47

NFL Championship Game 17

NFL championships 17

NFL records 13, 17, 24, 28, 32, 33, 39, 45

Offensive Rookie of the Year award 30, 43

Page, Alan 15, 17

Peterson, Adrian 43, 44, 45

playoffs 21, 24, 26, 28, 31, 33, 35, 37, 39, 43, 44, 47

Pro Bowl 43

Pro Football Hall of Fame 11

"Purple People Eaters" defensive line 15, 21, 43

Randle, John 31, 38

Rashad, Ahmad 25

Sharockman, Ed 10

Smith, Robert 28, 31, 33, 37

Steckel, Les 25

Stenerud, Jan 11

Stringer, Korey 41

Studwell, Scott 25

Super Bowl 11, 15, 17, 21, 22, 26, 27, 30, 33, 35, 47

Tarkenton, Fran 10, 14, 21, 27

team records 31, 39

Tice, Mike 37, 43

Tinglehoff, Mick 13

Van Brocklin, Norm 10, 14

Vikings name 9

Wilf, Zygi 16, 43

Williams, Kevin 37, 43

Williams, Pat 43

Wilson, Wade 26

Winfield, Antoine 43

Winter, Max 9, 14

Wright, Nate 22